Samuel
Morris

Samuel Morris

MEN OF FAITH

Samuel Morris

Lindley Baldwin

BETHANY HOUSE PUBLISHERS

MINNEAPOLIS, MINNESOTA 55438
A Division of Bethany Fellowship, Inc.

This special edition was printed for

BIBLE BELIEVERS FELLOWSHIP, INC.
P.O. BOX 0065 -- BALDWIN, NY 11510

Samuel Morris
Lindley Baldwin

Library of Congress Catalog Card Number 86-72978

ISBN 0-87123-950-7

Published by Bethany House Publishers
A Division of Bethany Fellowship, Inc.
6820 Auto Club Road, Minneapolis, Minnesota 55438

Printed in the United States of America

FOREWORD

Dr. Thaddeus C. Reade, who penned the first biographical sketch of Samuel Morris, once requested me to write a fuller and franker account of his life and work. Now, in my seventy-ninth year of a busy life, I have found time to comply with Dr. Reade's request. In the following pages I have drawn for minor details upon various writings subsequent to his. Among these I may mention "The Angel in Ebony" by Jorge O. Masa who kindly acknowledged my own contribution of original data to his volume.

I am thankful for the helpful suggestions of a number of friends including Dr. Robert Lee Stuart, President of Taylor University, and Dr. Elizabeth C. Bentley of its Faculty. I feel especially indebted to the late Dr. Harriet Stemen MacBeth, beloved teacher of Samuel Morris, who knew him better than anyone else.

The lengthening years since Dr. Reade commissioned me to this labor of love have but served to establish and enhance the reputation and influence of Samuel Morris; and I am now privileged to include striking proofs, hitherto unpublished, of the undying character of his spiritual leadership.

THE AUTHOR

A blinding light and an audible voice that seemed
to come from above commanded him to rise and flee.

PART I. THE JUNGLE PRINCE

A Pawn of War

The Dark Continent has given the world many of its most glittering jewels. But these diamonds do not shine when they are first discovered. They are only dull stones, and must be cut and ground before they glow with the colors of the rainbow.

Africa likewise has given to the world one of the most luminous leaders of modern times. As the diamond reflects the full splendor of the sun, so does the life of Samuel Morris reflect the undimmed glory of "the true Light" of the world. But the radiant power that made Samuel Morris an irresistible leader of men was not his by birth. It took divine cutting and grinding to fit this black diamond for its shining role.

No star of fortune shone down upon his cradle. He was merely one of thousands of native boys hidden in the jungles of Western Africa. His tribe was one of the Kru stock inhabiting the western forests of the Ivory Coast.

His name was Kaboo. His father was a tribal chieftain. But, though Kaboo was his eldest son and a prince in rank, no more wretched creature existed in the whole world. He had fallen from a position of freedom and honor to one of disgrace and worse than slavery.

In those regions it was the custom for a chief who was defeated in war to give his eldest son as a pawn or hostage to insure the payment of war indemnity. If payment lagged, he was often subjected to torture. Such was the fate of Kaboo.

While Kaboo was yet a child his father had twice been defeated in wars with neighboring tribes. Each time Kaboo had been put in pawn with the victorious chieftain. The first time occurred when Kaboo was too young to remember. His father was able to pay the indemnity promptly, and his son was soon restored to him. The second time Kaboo was held captive for several years before his father could complete his ransom. This had been an experience so dreadful that Kaboo would never speak of it.

He had been home only a short time when his tribe again became involved in a disastrous war. A coalition of enemies led by a cruel and depraved chief defeated Kaboo's people, laid waste their crops, and burned their village. His father was compelled to sue for peace and to pledge a much larger indemnity than his wasted territory could well afford to pay. Kaboo, who was now about fifteen years old, was put in pawn for the third time to insure the carrying out of this harsh treaty.

Kaboo's father came on the payment date with all the ivory, rubber, kola nuts, and other articles of trade his people had been able to gather together. The victorious chief took all that he brought and, after setting his own price upon it, declared that it did not fulfill the pledge. He refused to give up the pawn.

Kaboo's father was almost in despair. Yet he resolved to make one more effort. He induced his tribe to sacrifice their last belongings. When he came laden with goods upon his second visit, his offerings were again taken but again declared short of the balance due. For some years past his conqueror had been carrying on a thriving business with Sierra Leonian traders, with whom he exchanged his war booty for salt, trinkets, and rum—mostly rum. As his appetite for strong drink grew his idea of the exchange value of native currency diminished. No ransom payment was sufficient which did not keep him well supplied with liquor.

Knowing in advance the injustice of this drink-crazed chief, and fearing lest his son could not survive longer torture, Kaboo's father brought with him on his second visit one of his attractive daughters to put in the boy's place as a pawn.

Kaboo objected: "I can bear the punishment better than my sister. Let me remain." His father realized that further tribute was impossible. He could do nothing but return homeward with his daughter, leaving Kaboo to meet his certain fate.

When the father of Kaboo failed to come again, the infuriated chief ordered Kaboo to be whipped every day. Each beating was more prolonged and severe than the one before. A thorny poison vine was used as a whip. At each stroke it tore the flesh and implanted a fiery virus. The agonized victim felt as if his whole body were afire.

Each time the chieftain's executioner tormented Kaboo, a Kru slave, who was an eye-witness of the beating, was sent to Kaboo's father with a harrowing story of the ordeal, and a warning of worse to follow if he did not redouble his efforts to meet the full demands of his conqueror.

Kaboo's wounds did not have time to heal. The flesh of his back hung in shreds. Soon he became so exhausted from loss of blood and the fever induced by the poison vine that he could no longer stand or even sit up. A cross-tree was then erected and he was carried out and thrown over it while he was again beaten over his raw back.

The Miraculous Escape

Kaboo hoped that death would release

him before he met the awful fate of an un-
redeemed pawn. A number of Kaboo's
tribesmen had been taken as ordinary
slaves by this brutal chief. Several of them
had been accused as bewitchers. Kaboo had
seen them literally torn to pieces by drunk-
en and frenzied men. But he was now faced
by an even more diabolical fate.

Already, they had dug a pit in anticipa-
tion of the possible failure of his father to
return. If his final beating induced no further
payment, he was to be buried up to the neck.
His mouth would then be propped open, and
smeared with a sweet mixture to attract
the ants from a nearby ant-hill. The re-
sulting torment would merely prepare for
the final act when another type of insect—
the dreaded driver ants—would be permit-
ted to devour his living flesh bit by bit. After
the ants had cleaned his bones of every
particle of flesh, his white skeleton would
then be placed in front of his execution hut
as a gentle reminder to all future debtors.

As Kaboo was flung upon the cross-tree
for his final beating, all hope as well as
physical strength left him. He longed only
for the boon of death.

Then, suddenly, something very strange
happened. A great light like a flash of light-
ning broke over him. The light blinded all
about him. An audible voice that seemed
to come from above commanded him to rise

and flee. All heard the voice and saw the light but saw no man.

At the same time there occurred one of those instantaneous healings which science can neither deny nor explain. In the twinkling of an eye Kaboo found his strength restored. He had had nothing to eat or drink all that day. Yet he felt neither hunger nor thirst nor weakness. Leaping up, he obeyed the mysterious voice and fled from the astonished natives with the speed of a deer.

What was the source of the mysterious light that had brought him new strength and freedom? Kaboo did not know or suspect. He had never heard of the Christian God. He knew nothing of special acts of Divine Providence. He had never heard of a Saviour who had once been put in pawn, a ransom for many. The earthly prince who had just hung over a cross-tree of torture did not dream of a heavenly Prince who had been mocked and beaten as a prisoner and had suffered a degraded death by slow torture upon a tree.

But Kaboo did know that some strange and invisible power had come to his rescue. At one moment he had been too ill to sit erect and now he was running away at top speed.

It was on a Friday that he made his escape. Kaboo never forgot that day. He called it his Deliverance Day, and as long

as he lived he always celebrated that day
of the week by fasting, taking neither food
nor water.

The Kindly Light

Kaboo hid in the hollow of a tree until
nightfall to elude his pursuers. When night
came Kaboo realized that he had escaped
one kind of death only to plunge into another
deadly hazard. He was alone in the jungle
where no unaided man could hope to survive for long. Worst of all, he was not only
without friends and weapons, but also without home or destination!

He dared not return to his own tribe and
family. To do so would bring upon his people
the bitter revenge of their enraged conqueror. He dared not be seen by a native
of another tribe lest he be returned to his
former captor for the large reward usually
paid for an escaped pawn.

In the midst of his new despair, another
marvel appeared. In those regions the
dense forests are dark even during the day;
at night they are impossible to penetrate.
But the same friendly light that had flooded
the scene of his intended execution shone
again around him. Wandering in another
wilderness, a company of liberated bonds-
men long ago enjoyed a similar guidance
when "the Lord went before them by day

in a pillar of a cloud, to lead them the way;
and by night in a pillar of fire, to give them
light." Whether it was an external light or
a mental illumination that guided Kaboo,
his pathway was made clear.

And he needed such light quite as much
as did the children of Israel. Poisonous
cobras, puffadders, and vipers lay in wait
along Kaboo's pathway. The great python
hung overhead. But more than the glaring
eyes of leopards and the stings of poisonous
serpents he had to fear his own kind. In
the forests of this vast region lived some
of the most savage races in the world.
Cannibalism was still widely practiced.

But through all these obstacles and dan-
gers the kindly light led Kaboo. By its aid
he could see at night to gather fruits and
roots for nourishment, and to cross lakes
and rivers where luminous eyes betrayed
the lurking crocodiles.

During the day-times he continued to
hide in tree trunks to avoid village outposts.
After travelling many nights Kaboo arrived
at a plantation on the outskirts of a town
beside a river. Up to this time he had not
met a single human being. No human guide
had directed him through the wilderness to
this spot.

At his first glance he saw that this was
not a native village but some kind of foreign
settlement peculiar to the white man. He

would have been afraid to approach their
buildings if he had not seen one of his own
Kru race busy at work in the distance. Kaboo approached him and learned to his joy
that he had come into the hands not of slave-
traders but slave-liberators. The mysterious light had led him to a settlement near
Monrovia, the capital of Liberia.

To appreciate this third manifestation of
divine favor, one must recall that almost
the whole of Liberia at that time was still
a wilderness under the domination of jungle
law. Even as late as 1934 a League of Nations Committee reported that in Liberia
many children were still given as pawns
for sums which their parents could not re-
deem. When Kaboo reached Monrovia it
was the only important stronghold of civ-
ilized law. Thus, Kaboo had been led to the
one community out of thousands where he
was to be really safe.

Kaboo emerged from the forest to safety
on Friday, his original Deliverance Day,
weeks after he had first made his escape
from death.

A New Name

He sought employment and found it on
the coffee plantation where the other Kru
boy was working. For his labor he was
given a bunk in the barracks, his board,

and such cheap clothing as was worn by the natives laborers.

His Kru companion had been listening to the missionaries and had learned to pray. Kaboo saw him on his knees, both hands lifted up and face upturned. When Kaboo asked him what he was doing, he replied, "I am talking to God."

"Who is your God," asked Kaboo.

"He is my Father," answered the boy.

"Then you are talking to your Father," said Kaboo. Ever afterward he called praying, "talking to my Father." To his child-like faith, prayer was a simple and as sure as conversing with an earthly parent.

The next Sunday Kaboo was invited to attend church. He found a crowd gathered around a woman who was speaking through an interpreter. She was telling them about the conversion of Saul; how a light from heaven suddenly shone upon him and a mysterious voice spoke from above.

Kaboo cried out: "That's just what I saw! I have seen that light! That is the same light that saved me and brought me here!" Kaboo had been wondering all the time why he had been so marvellously saved from death and guided through the forest. Now, in a flash he began to understand.

God cannot save a soul until that soul has knowledge of Him and exercises conscious faith. But the Providence of God often spares the lives and heals the bodies of those who are yet strangers to Him, either in answer to the prayers of believers or for His own good purposes.

But, Kaboo was still blind to the meaning of salvation as was Saul when he was stricken on the way to Damascus. Saul needed some believer to instruct him. Just as the divine command came to Ananias, so the responsibility for the enlightenment of Kaboo was placed upon this missionary from whom he had just heard of the conversion of Saul of Tarsus.

She was Miss Knolls, formerly a resident of Ft. Wayne, Indiana. She had been educated at Taylor University which was then located in that city and known as Ft. Wayne College. She had just come to Liberia. Many others later helped to instruct Kaboo, but it was Miss Knolls who guided him into God's Kingdom, and awakened him to his true mission in life.

Kaboo became a regular attendant at the religious services and classes conducted by Miss Knolls. She gave him his first elementary lessons in reading and writing the English language. Little by little, he learned the beautiful story of Jesus' birth in a manger; His ministry to the humble, the sinful, and the diseased; His atoning death and resurrection. Kaboo readily accepted this new-found Saviour of souls as the same "Unknown God" who had previously saved his body.

But Kaboo was not satisfied. He was beginning to wish that he could be like the saintly missionary. He longed to be able to preach to his own Kru people in their own language the same glad tidings of God's love which had brought peace to his own soul. But, he felt his utter lack of fitness and authority for such a mission in life.

Like every Christian convert Kaboo soon became conscious that redemption from the guilt and penalty of past sins does not free from the dominion of future sins through the weakness of the flesh. His flesh bore the stripes of his many beatings as a pawn, and his mind had naturally been habituated to fear and hate during years of cruel suffering. The degradation he had undergone gave him a hopeless feeling of inferiority. Ignorant and outcast, he could see no future for himself short of another miracle.

Kaboo did not know that God has provided just such another miracle for every believer through the work of the Holy Spirit. For redemption is by power as well as blood, and it is the power of the Spirit that purifies the heart of all bitterness, and commissions and endows the believer for efficient service to God. Kaboo had never heard of this divine Helper who comes in His fullness only after conversion, when the believer is conscious of his defects and ready to consecrate his life wholly to God.

But the Holy Spirit who is also the very Spirit of Truth came to the aid of poor Kaboo. For, it is the mission of this Helper to give "first aid" to all honest seekers, "For we know not what we should pray for as we ought; but the Spirit himself maketh intercession for us with groanings which cannot be uttered."

So, Kaboo was encouraged to keep "talking to his Father" night after night when his work was done. He wrestled in prayer with such an agonized voice and made so much disturbance in the bunk-house that his fellow-workers finally reached the end of their patience. They warned him that he would have to keep still or seek other quarters. Kaboo went into the woods to pray.

He remained in the forest one night until after midnight. Later he related what happened: "I went to my bunk, weary and heavyhearted, and lay down to rest. My tongue was still, but my heart went on praying. All at once my room grew light! At first I thought the sun was rising, but the others all around me were sound asleep. The room grew lighter till it was full of glory. The burden of my heart suddenly disappeared and I was filled with a sense of inner joy.

"My body felt as light as a feather. I was filled with a power that made me feel

that I could almost fly. I could not contain
my joy but shouted until everyone in the
barracks was awakened. There was no
more sleep there that night. Some thought
I had gone crazy; others, that a devil had
gotten into me. But I knew my own heart.
This was my adoption. I was now a son of
the heavenly King. I knew then that my
Father had saved me for a purpose, and
that He would work with me.''

This was that complete and harmonious
union with God through the Holy Spirit that
equipped Kaboo with superhuman power
for victorious leadership. Kaboo never
spoke of this glorious event as his conversion. He always called it his ''adoption.''
Though he had no knowledge of Greek, he
used this word in the same sense as did
the learned Paul in his letter to the Ephe-
sians—one who is already a weak, minor
child of God is at last placed in the position
of a trusted adult son with whom God will
commune and cooperate fully.

But Kaboo did not reason all this out.
He knew nothing about the Holy Spirit in
theology. He was filled with God's Spirit
simply because he was willing to yield himself wholly to God. He sought after God just
as a hungry boy seeks for food; and, because he hungered for righteousness, God
sent down his own transforming and em-

powering Spirit in answer to that childlike faith.

Kaboo was taken into the Methodist Church and baptized under the name of Samuel Morris. This name was chosen by Miss Knolls in honor of her benefactor, Samuel Morris, who was a banker of Fort Wayne, Indiana. Mr. Morris had assisted Miss Knolls to prepare for the work of preaching the Gospel. Kaboo was the first fruit of her missionary labor, and she named him "Samuel Morris" in gratitude. In doing so she little guessed that this dark namesake would confer the greatest honor upon the name of her benefactor.

First Signs of Leadership

Samuel Morris lived in Liberia for some two years after his baptism. He left the plantation and worked in Monrovia at odd jobs such as house painting. He helped to paint Liberia College. His earnings were barely enough to keep him alive, but Sammy was happy. He was so interested in religion that he sought out and talked to every missionary in that region.

He did much work for the missionaries. He learned many of their religious songs by heart, and could sing them with wonderful effect although he did not know the meaning of some of the words. Soon he earned the reputation of being the most consecrated and zealous Christian in that part of Liberia.

Not long after his own conversion he led another young boy to accept Christ as his Saviour. By a remarkable coincidence this African was an escaped slave who had been held by the same cruel chieftain to whom Samuel had been last in pawn. This slave had been present at the final torture of Kaboo, and had seen the mysterious flash of light and heard the voice commanding Kaboo to flee.

An ordinary slave was of little value compared to a chief's pawn. Hence, it had been comparatively easy for him to escape, and to travel safely by day along a conventional route. He was baptized under the name of Henry O'Neil. He confirmed the testimony of Kaboo regarding his miraculous escape from pawn. Their joint testimony made a great impression upon people of Monrovia.

Already, Samuel Morris began to show that amazing power of spiritual leadership that was to win him fame in later years. The following incident shows his unique method of influencing others, not by sermons or arguments or by any human force, but simply by invoking the Holy Spirit to act for him.

Three women in Monrovia agreed to conduct prayer-meetings lasting from midnight to daylight. In this way they sought to bring a spiritual awakening to the entire community. But they lacked a convert whose example might encourage the others. One night a boy entered. He prayed for hours, prostrated before the pulpit. The women, supposing him to be a new convert, hurried out to bring the good news to others. When they returned they found that the boy was Samuel Morris. He was praying not for himself but for others. His prayers were heard. Soon fifty young people accepted Christ at the following meetings.

Rev. C. E. Smirl, a missionary to Liberia, told Sammy that he needed an education in order to become an effective minister to his own people, and that such an education must be acquired in America. Altough Sammy did not possess a cent of money he hoped that the Lord would somehow provide the hundred dollars needed to take him across the ocean. But his final determination to go to America was caused by a desire for something far more important than book learning.

The sermons of the missionaries to people like himself had been quite elementary. They stressed salvation through faith in the Lord Jesus Christ, but revealed little about the specific person and unique function of the Comforter. One day a Spirit-filled missionary read to Sammy the 14th chapter of St. John in which the Savior first announced to His assembled disciples the coming of a new and powerful Helper, the Holy Ghost. Already, Sammy had experienced the blessing of this divine Spirit in his heart; but this was the first time his head had been introduced to the name and full significance of the Holy Spirit.

When he first understood that this Spirit works here on earth, and is an actual, living Person, he had no words adequate to express his wonderment and happiness. He found it easy to attribute the mysterious voice that had led to his escape from pawn to God's Spirit who spoke to him, as to Samuel of old, ere he yet knew the voice of the Lord. He made long journeys to talk to missionaries about the Holy Ghost. The 14th chapter of St. John became Sammy's constant study.

He came so often to visit the missionaries and asked so many hard questions about the Spirit that one was finally compelled to confess: "I have told you everything I know about the Holy Ghost." But he persisted, "Who told you what you know about the Holy Ghost?" She replied that she owed most of her understanding of this subject to Stephen Merritt, who was then home secretary to Bishop William Taylor.

Samuel Morris then asked, "Where is Stephen Merritt?"

The missionary replied: "In New York."

Samuel Morris promptly declared, "I will go to see him!"

Without further ceremony he started on his way, running directly to the sea coast. He no longer bothered his head about getting the hundred dollars for the passage money. The Holy Spirit was more important than money; He would provide the way. When he arrived, a sailing ship was anchored in the offing. He was filled with joy. His Father had answered his prayers.

A small boat put out from the ship and came ashore bearing the captain and some of the crew. When the captain stepped ashore to attend to the loading of the cargo, he was confronted by an unattractive black boy, who said: "My Father told me you would take me to New York to see Stephen Merritt."

The captain said, "Where is your father?"

Samuel Morris replied, "In heaven."

The captain was a very gruff man. He said, with an oath, "My ship does not carry passengers. You must be crazy."

Samuel Morris stood guard near the small boat all day. That night, when the captain returned to the boat, Samuel Morris

again beseeched him to take him to New
York. The captain threatened to kick him,
and the boat returned to the ship without
him. But Samuel continued to believe in his
Father's promise. He slept on the sand
where the small boat had landed, and
prayed again most of the night. The next
day he was again refused, but such was his
faith that he would not leave the beach although he had had nothing to eat for two
days. Next morning was Sunday. The captain and crew came again to shore. When
the captain stepped ashore this time, the
Kru boy hurried up to him, saying: "My
Father told me last night that you would
take me this time."

The captain looked at him in amaze-
ment. Two of the crew had deserted the ship
the previous night, leaving him short-
handed. He recognized that Sammy was a
Kru and assumed that he was an experienced sailor, as were so many of his coun-
try-men. "How much pay do you want,"
he asked. "Just take me to New York to
see Stephen Merritt," replied Sammy. The
captain turned to the boat crew and told
them to take the boy out to the ship.

Samuel Morris was delighted. His
prayers had been granted. He was on board
a ship bound for America.

PART II.
VOYAGE AND CONQUEST

A Columbus of the Spirit

It is safe to say that Samuel Morris was the first explorer to sail the Atlantic in quest of the riches of the Holy Spirit. The new world discovered by Columbus was only an extension of the old world of perishable physical things. Samuel Morris adventured forth to find the new world of the Spirit which will endure in the "new earth" yet to be.

His own voyage was to prove as dangerous and thrilling as that of Christopher Columbus. He was to spend nearly a half year aboard that vessel, and to pass through many perils before he reached his goal. The ship was a tramp vessel owned by its captain. He intended to put in much time in coast-wise trading with the Africans before he steered for America with a full cargo.

On boarding the vessel Sammy found a young man lying helpless on the deck. He had been serving as cabin-boy for the captain. He had been severely injured, and was unable to walk. The black boy knelt down beside him and prayed for him. The young man immediately arose and walked. Divine healing had made him every whit whole!

This grateful youth learned that Samuel had not eaten since Thursday evening. It was then Sunday noon. Sammy was led to the mess room, but the cook refused to serve him because he was a Negro and no orders to feed him had been given by the captain. However, Sammy's new-found friend managed to secure food for himself and shared it liberally with his dusky benefactor.

When the captain came out to the ship that night, he questioned Samuel and soon found that he was a complete land-lubber. He was told that he would have to be put ashore at once because he would probably be seasick all the time and unable to work. The ship was a three hundred and fifty foot three-master, and a very rough-riding vessel.

Sammy assured the captain that he would not get sick, and would work for him every day until he reached New York. The young man who had been healed through Sammy's prayers then came up and begged: "Please take him, captain. Look what he has done for me!" That night they weighed anchor and the Kru boy was on his way to a new world.

Life aboard this ship was a continuous round of cruelty. Almost every word was accompanied by an oath, a kick, or a cuff. The captain was a hard bargainer and a

harsh master. He did much business with
the Arab traders when they came to the
coast. Here it was a case of "Greek meeting
Greek," an eye for an eye and a tooth for
a tooth. The captain had been hardened in
such ruthless encounters. Life or death was
at his command aboard his ship. All lived
in dread of him.

The crew was a motley group picked up
in the four quarters of the globe. Sammy
was the only one of his race aboard ship,
and the whole crew resented his presence
and began to plan to do away with him.
Blows and abuses were rained on his head
from all sides.

On their third night out Sammy was
lashed to a spar in the ship's rigging where
he could help reef the sails and pull the
ropes. That night a tropical storm came up
suddenly and caught the ship with all can-
vas spread. She was lightly laden. There
was no time to reef the sails. They had to
ride out the storm. Sammy prayed:
"Father, I am not afraid, for I know that
you will take care of me. But, I don't like
to be on the mast. Won't you please make
it so that I won't have to come up here."
He felt assured that his prayer would be
answered, but his faith was sorely tried.

The spar on which he was bound was
often under water or drenched with spray.
Sammy swallowed so much sea water that

be became deathly ill. When he was at last
untied and brought down to the foot of the
mast, he fell in a heap. The captain came
up to him and kicked him. The deck was
still awash and the ship was rolling and
pitching heavily. Sammy got to his knees,
sick as he was, and with uplifted hands
prayed: "Father, you know I promised to
work for this man every day till I got to
America. I cannot work when I am sick like
this. Please take away this sickness." Then
he rose to his feet and resumed his tasks.
He was never ill again on that ship.

The next day, when he was about to go
aloft, the cabin-boy came up to him, saying,
"Sam, I heard you praying during that
storm. I don't like it below the decks, and
you are not trained to work in rigging. Let's
trade places." Sammy accepted his offer,
and another prayer had been answered.

When Sammy reported to the captain for
duty, the latter was drunk. He registered
his disgust by striking Sammy with his fist,
knocking him to the floor unconscious.
When Sammy regained consciousness the
captain had sobered somewhat. Sammy got
up and started about his work as cheerfully
as if nothing had happened. He asked the
captain if he knew about Jesus. Vague
memories of his mother and childhood days
stirred in the brutalized mind of the

mariner. Sammy knelt down and prayed for the captain with such sincerity and fervor that he was moved to bow his head in spite of himself. It was the beginning of a period of conviction.

However, there was little time for meditation just then. The severe storm that had just passed had badly wrenched the superstructure of the ship. The hull had opened many seams and was leaking badly. A small island was sighted nearby, and they anchored to leeward to make repairs.

While the carpenters and caulkers were busy, the rest of the crew had to man the pumps to keep the ship afloat. Sammy was posted at one of the pumps which must be kept going night and day. The task was a hard one for an able-bodied, seasoned sailor. Sammy was a small, frail boy in his teens. Yet he was forced to pump along with the strongest. He pumped and prayed, and prayed and pumped.

The crew were furnished rum to keep up their courage and deaden the pains of fatigue. Sammy was offered rum also, but he said that his Father in heaven would give him strength. For two weeks they pumped. Sammy's strength was tried to the fainting point, but the Holy Spirit gave him the strength and endurance he lacked by nature.

Mastering a Brutal Seaman

When they hoisted anchor again for the open sea it was a day of general rejoicing. The captain issued an extra ration of rum to all hands. They were filled and fired with the crude liquor. Late in the afternoon, a free-for-all fight started aft. It was a meaningless brawl caused by a flaring up of racial prejudices. A big Malay, who thought himself insulted, seized a cutlass and rushed at some of his shipmates with murder in his heart. Sammy stepped between the Malay and his intended victims and said in his quiet way: "Don't kill, don't kill."

As it happened, this very Malay had boasted to the crew that he intended to kill Sammy. He had a special hatred for all Negroes. His cutlass had been fatal to many Africans in previous encounters. He was a killer of the most dangerous type. Even the captain kept shy of him.

As Sammy advanced to meet him, he raised his weapon and scowled at the boy as if he would cut him to pieces. Here was his opportunity to make good his threat. But Sammy looked him straight in the eye, and made no movement to defend himself. The Malay slowly lowered his weapon, and went back to his bunk. This Godless ruffian was face to face with a power stronger than man.

As Sammy advanced to meet him, he raised his weapon and scowled at the boy as if he could cut him to pieces.

At that moment the captain, hearing the turmoil, came on deck with a pistol in each hand ready to shoot down the trouble-makers. When he saw that the crew had suddenly stopped fighting because Sammy had interceded, he could not but recognize that this African boy possessed a mysterious power that was stronger than the animal passions of the most brutal of men. He went below deck with Sammy who dropped to his knees and prayed for the entire crew. For the first time the captain joined in prayer, a prayer of thanksgiving that the Lord had sent such an ambassador of peace among them. In that moment he repented of his sins and found newness of life. He was but the first of many Christian converts to be made by Sammy aboard that ship.

Sammy found the captain's cabin a dark and dismal den. It had been the scene of many orgies. The accumulation of many years of smoke, dust, and filth was apparent on every side. Sammy gave that cabin a baptism of soap and water. Even the deadly weapons that hung on the walls became shining decorations under his care. One of Sammy's sayings was, "The Spirit will not dwell where filth abides." The captain was pleased, and showed his "new quarters" to the ship's officers.

Gradually, Sammy won the captain's heart completely. At first he had been annoyed by Sammy's frequent prayers; now, he stood silently, cap in hand, while Sammy prayed. Under this new influence, the captain no longer paid his crew with rum. Serious fights among the crew ceased. Now, the captain would call his crew to quarters for prayers. On such occasions Sammy's clear, strong voice and the songs he had learned by heart while in Liberia, played a great part in winning the good will of the crew. Captain and crew when off duty would sit for hours and listen to him sing those beautiful, soul-stirring religious songs which never lost their power and charm. As Sammy would sing, voice after voice would catch up the melody of the chorus until all would come under the spell of the tender passion of man's eternal quest for God, and sense the wonder of His answering grace.

The cut-throat Malay who had threatened Samuel Morris took dangerously ill. He sank so low that all hope was abandoned for his recovery. Sammy did not know his language, and had nothing in common with him. But when he heard of his illness, he went to his bunk and prayed for him. He was healed. This burly ruffian had known no God, and had lived only for the lusts of the flesh. He had hated the Negro race, and never lost an opportunity to show it. All that was now changed. The Malay would have given his life for this black boy.

The crew as a whole were without ideals, and had no common ground of affinity, being recruited from all parts of the world. Each lip proclaimed a different tongue. Each heart recalled a different home. But now all prayed and sang with Samuel Morris. Differences of race, country, language, and creed were forgotten. Sammy's God became their God. The Light that had brought him to them shone through him so radiantly that all could see it, and seeing it found a new bond of brotherhood.

A Bloody Battle

The captain's trade with the people on mainland and islands was unusually profitable. The ship was nearly loaded with African products. A few more stops, and the captain would be ready to steer straight for New York. Sammy was beginning to enjoy the voyage.

Late one evening they sighted a large island or peninsula the name of which Sammy never learned. Next morning the captain decided to go ashore with a stock of merchandise with which to barter. He loaded the ship's boat heavily and took along a larger boat crew than usual. Something seemed to tell him that all was not well. He had armed his men and instructed the lookout in the crow's nest to scan the shore carefully at all times with his marine glasses, and to wig-wag him if anything unusual took place on shore. The boat was so heavily loaded that it was slow going against the tide. When it was about halfway between the ship and shore, the lookout saw hundreds of people approaching the beach carrying long, light, narrow boats which they shot out into the sea like so many arrows. The lookout signalled the captain to return to the ship.

The captain started back but his loaded craft was no match for the long, light boats. Soon they were close astern and some, shooting close alongside, prevented the crew from using their oars. The natives did not expect a fight. They were bent upon capturing the boat, the ship, and its entire cargo without a struggle. Their leader was a renegade white man. Some weeks before this time he had led his followers in a successful mass attack upon an outbound trading ship loaded with rum and other goods. The captain of that vessel, finding himself surrounded by a ruse, had given up the ship in the hope of saving the lives of himself and the crew. The ship was looted. Soon the looters became a drunken mob. With the consent of their leader the captain and every member of his crew were compelled to walk the plank.

Emboldened by that success, they now hoped to repeat their maneuver. But Sammy's captain was shrewd enough to take advantage of their overconfidence. As they swarmed around, he and his crew opened fire upon them at such close range that every shot took its toll. Having thrown them into a panic, the boat crew fought its way within gunshot of the ship. The crew on the ship then poured a withering fire into the attackers. The captain and crew managed to climb aboard, though they could not hoist the boat.

But while the ship's crew were engaged in the rescue of the captain and his boat crew, another group headed by their white leader began to board the ship on the farther side. The vessel was heavily laden and riding low. They had made boarding ladders of ropes, and were soon fastening them to the rail of the ship on every side. Their leader was among the first to reach the deck. He spoke English. Approaching the captain he shouted a demand for the surrender of the ship. But the ship's crew had had time to make preparations for the expected battle. Armed men had been posted high up in the rigging. One of these shot the leader and he was thrown overboard. Some of his followers, however, dashed for the hatch and reached the hold of the ship, expecting to loot it.

Sammy was standing by the captain's side when the renegade white man was shot. When the captain saw the natives going into the hold of the ship, he ordered Sammy to go to his cabin, lock and bolt the door on the inside, and guard the ship's valuables. He hoped this plan would also keep Sammy out of harm's way.

The crew fastened down the hatches so that those already in the hold could not get out. Then the crew turned their attention to the others who by this time were swarming onto the deck from all sides. Sammy could see no more of the fighting, but he could hear the crack of the guns, the thud of men falling to the deck, and the cries and groans of the wounded. It was a fight to the death. No quarter was asked and none given. About midday a stiff breeze sprang up, and the ship began to roll so that it could no longer be boarded. The gunfire ceased. Soon Sammy could hear the click, click of the anchor chains as they wound round the capstan. The ship began to move. For hours afterward, he could hear the tramp of heavy, booted feet on the deck, and then the splash of bodies falling into the sea. It was nightfall before Sammy heard the hatches opening and the crew coming down into the hold of the ship to seize looters who had imbibed their fill of rum and were easily overcome.

The captain then went to his cabin and signalled Sammy to unlock the door. When the door swung open, the captain staggered into the room more dead than alive. He was completely exhausted from loss of blood and the long, terrific struggle. He sank to the floor in a faint. Sammy pulled him into his bunk, and bathed and dressed his wounds as best he could. Then he kneeled down beside the bed and poured out his very soul in prayer for his friend.

The captain revived while Sammy was praying. He put his arm gently around the Negro's bare shoulders and drew him closer, saying: "Sammy! your prayers have saved us and the ship. Our men fought like demons, but we were out-numbered, ten to one. Few of the enemy had firearms, but they all had knives or war clubs. If the wind had not sprung up so that the ship rolled and dragged her anchors, they would have swarmed over us like ants."

The next morning was a sad one for all aboard ship. Many of the crew had been severely wounded, and several had been killed. The decks were stained with blood. Sammy's grief was heavy when he saw the bodies of friends whom he had learned to love dropped into the sea. But he was soon too busy for sorrow. To the living he became physician, nurse, and comforter throughout the remainder of the voyage. His cheerfulness and his complete faith in God's Providence soon transformed the spirit of the ship. All went about their tasks willingly without the usual oaths and cuffs.

New York Bows to Sammy

When at last the tramp ship reached New York, Sammy had been aboard about five months. He had come aboard in jumper and overalls without shoes. He had worked for his passage. The crew took up a collection of clothing, and pieced together a suit for him with cap and shoes so that he could go ashore decently dressed.

Sammy was all excitement as the harbor was sighted. Hardships and suffering were all forgotten. Everyone aboard that ship was now his friend, the once bloodthirsty Malay the fondest of all. As they all shook hands with Sammy for the last time many of these hardened men wept like children. Racial barriers were forgotten; they had found a bond of affection stronger than the accident of birth. God's dark-skinned ambassador had dwelt among them. Through him they had come to realize that there is a personal, prayer-answering God who is no respecter of race or color.

It was again Friday, Sammy's original Deliverance Day, when the ship was warped into her dock at the foot of Pike

Street on the East River. When the gang
plank was lowered, Samuel Morris was the
first one to go down it. A man was just
passing as he reached the dock. Sammy
at once hailed the stranger with the ques-
tion, "Where can I find Stephen Merritt?"

The passer-by had partaken of Stephen
Merritt's hospitality at his mission. He
promptly answered, "I know him; he lives
away over on Eighth Avenue—on the other
side of town. I'll take you to him for a dollar."

The ship had docked more than three
miles from the Bethel in a district where
Rev. Stephen Merritt was unknown. Had it
not been for the guidance of the Holy Spirit
and Sammy's faith in his mission, it might
have proved difficult for him to find Mr.
Merritt.

Sammy had not a penny to his name,
but he accepted the tramp's offer in the
serene faith that the dollar would somehow
be produced. The tramp led Sammy along
many streets and through great crowds of
busy, hurrying people. It was getting dark
when they reached Mr. Merritt. He had
closed the office and was just locking the
door when they came up. The guide said,
"There is Stephen Merritt, that man who
is putting the key in the door."

Sammy ran forward, exclaiming: "I
am Samuel Morris. I have just come from

Africa to talk with you about the Holy Ghost."

Merritt was both amazed and amused at this odd greeting. He asked Sammy if he had any letters of introduction.

"No, I had no time to wait," replied Sammy.

Stephen Merritt kindly told Sammy that an appointment at that hour did not leave a moment's time to talk to him, but that if he would step into the mission next door and wait, his entertainment for the night would be arranged.

Sammy started for the mission when the tramp who had guided him called out, "Where is my dollar?" Sammy, who never doubted the Providence of his heavenly Father, merely waved his hand in the direction of Stephen Merritt, saying, "Stephen Merritt pays all my bills now." Merritt smilingly handed over the dollar to the tramp and entered his coach.

Stephen Merritt kept his appointment and then went home. As he was leaving his coach, he suddenly remembered the African boy and had his coachman drive him back to the Bethel. He found Samuel Morris surrounded by seventeen men prostrate on their faces before him. He had just told them about Jesus and they were rejoicing in His pardon. On his first night in America this young African who could scarcely

Sammy is taken in by Mr. Stephen Merritt.

speak our language had brought nearly a
score of souls to Christ! When the group had
been dismissed, Stephen Merritt, who was
deeply moved by this extraordinary sight,
took Sammy home with him in his coach.
It was his first ride in a coach and behind
a fine team of prancing horses. He was
thrilled. Such a team of well matched and
finely gaited horses is a beautiful sight for
any eyes. But to this Kru boy, reared in
the jungle and gifted with an unspoiled in-
stinct for the natural beauty of living things,
these spirited horses were delightful beyond
words. Merritt could hardly coax him away
from them after they had arrived.

Stephen Merritt was a wealthy man and
lived in a veritable palace in Hoboken
Heights, then an aristocratic section. It
was one o'clock in the morning when they
reached his residence. His faithful wife
had waited up for him. When he opened the
door she asked, "Why, what have you here,
Stephen?"

Merritt answered, "Oh, Dolly, this is an
angel in ebony!"

Mrs. Merritt still astonished, gasped:
"What are you going to do with him?"

"I am going to put him in the bishop's
bed," replied Merritt.

"Oh, no! Don't do that!" she objected.
But he did. Up they went to the bedroom
which had been set apart as the lodging-

place of Bishop William Taylor whenever
he was in New York. There Merritt showed
Sammy, who had never slept in a real
bed, how to open and get into one, how to
light the gas and to turn it out. He even
brought out one of the bishop's own night-
gowns and put it on Sammy. The bishop
was a large man and his voluminous gown
made Sammy look so funny that Merritt
again enjoyed a hearty laugh.

But his laughter was soon changed to
deep emotion. Sammy pushed up the long
sleeves of his gown and, extending his hand
to his host, asked him to kneel with him
in prayer. The soul of Samuel Morris was
on fire. The light that had led him so far
from home was to be shared with his host
that night. This man who had been preaching the Gospel for years received a new
visitation of the Holy Spirit. In those few
moments of prayer uttered by an unlettered
Negro, the man whom Bishop Taylor had
selected as his secretary had a revelation
of the reality and power of the Comforter
such as he had never known before.

When Sammy awoke the next morning
he hurriedly made up his bed, tidied the
room, and then found his way down to the
stables. There he immediately went to
work, helping the groom care for the
horses. Stephen Merritt rose late. He went
to the bishop's room, but the "angel in

ebony" was not there. When at last he was
found at work in the stable he was brought
into the house by Mr. Merritt and introduced to his family. Breakfast was just
ready.

It was the first time that Stephen Merritt and the members of his household had
ever sat down to eat with a Negro. How
it had come about was a mystery to them.
The experience was equally new to Sammy
who had never eaten at the same table with
white people. It was also his first meal in
America. He had to be shown how to eat
the strange food. Under Mr. Merritt's kindly directions he did justice to the fine meal.
He was hungry enough, having had nothing
to eat from Thursday evening till late that
Saturday morning.

A Funeral Becomes a Revival!

Stephen Merritt was a very busy man.
His time was taken up with his church work.
That Saturday morning he had to conduct
the funeral of a prominent man in Harlem.
He took Sammy along with him in the
coach. On his way he stopped to pick up
two eminent divines who were to assist him
with the funeral services. When the first of
these doctors of divinity looked into the
coach and saw a black boy sitting there,
the minister started to draw back. He

waited a moment, expecting the shabby youth to get out. When they finally got in, they were plainly shocked to be obliged to ride with this humble African. They said nothing but cast glances in his direction that spoke their disapproval.

It was embarrassing to Rev. Stephen Merritt. As a diversion he tried to entertain Sammy by pointing out all the interesting places they were passing such as Central Park, the Grand Opera House, and other notable sights. But Sammy was interested in something even more wondrous than the wonders of this great city. Putting his black hand on Merritt's knee, he said, "'Did you ever pray while riding in a coach?" Merritt answered that he had frequently had blessed times while riding about in a coach, but that he had never engaged in formal prayers.

Sammy said, "We will pray." And they did. It was the first time that Stephen Merritt had ever kneeled down in a coach to pray. Sammy began at once: "Father, I have been months coming to see Stephen Merritt so that I could talk to him about the Holy Ghost. Now that I am here, he shows me the harbor, the churches, the banks and other buildings, but does not say a word about this Spirit I am so anxious to know more about. Fill him with Thyself so that he will not think, or talk, or write, or preach about anything but Thee and the Holy Ghost."

What happened in that coach was no ordinary manifestation of divine favor. Stephen Merritt had participated in the consecration of many missionaries, the ordination of many ministers, the installation of bishops, and the laying on of hands by holy people. But he had never experienced the burning presence of the Holy Spirit as he did while he was kneeling in that coach, beside Sammy Morris who was penniless and clad in tattered garments. Merritt's whole life was changed in that amazing moment.

When they began their ride these reverend gentlemen had been a little ashamed to be seen riding with such a ragged Negro. After Sammy's prayer service, it was they who felt ashamed of their own spiritual shabbiness. They felt that Sammy's outer garb should be more in harmony with his inner grace. So, at Merritt's suggestion they stopped at a clothing store to buy a new outfit for their guest.

Stephen Merritt told the storekeeper that "nothing was too good" for this boy. He then stepped aside to send a message. The storekeeper took his directions literally, aided and abetted by the two clergymen who were Methodist ministers. Later, Stephen Merritt jestingly remarked:

"Where two or more Methodist preachers are gathered together, they cannot be outdone in generosity when they can get someone else to foot the bill." In this case the two ministers certainly vied with one another in outfitting Sammy with the best clothing in the store. When Stephen Merritt rejoined them, he found Samuel trying to recognize himself in a mirror which reflected the heart of Africa in the fashion of Fifth Avenue. Merritt smilingly paid the goodly bill. In fact, even the queer old clothes there discarded by Samuel seemed precious in his eyes. He saved and exhibited them in his office for many years afterward.

After Sammy had been clothed in fine style, they drove directly to the funeral. A great many people came to honor the dead. Stephen Merritt had expected a large gathering and had carefully prepared his funeral sermon. But that prayer in the coach had given him a new spirit. Old things had passed away. People marveled at the sermon he preached that day.

The very heavens seemed to open as he forgot his formal speech and poured forth a message of tender sympathy inspired by the Comforter Himself. The other two ministers felt the same divine inspiration. In their shorter tributes they spoke with such power that, as they remarked afterward, they were surprised at their own eloquence.

The people listened in a rapture, little dreaming that these gifted orators were but the medium through which a poor, black boy had turned a scene of mourning into one of joy. Though it was his faith that had brought the unction from on high Samuel said not a word during the services. He simply sat there, so filled with the Spirit that in a vision he seemed to see all the way to the threshold of heaven. He could feel the touch of angelic wings.

He felt the beauty of this solemn Christian ceremony in contrast to former scenes of savage brutality. He had seen his own people slaughtered like cattle and left without burial. He remembered the depraved rites of the Leopard Worshippers. He had seen other pawns and slaves tortured and killed with never a word of comfort spoken at their burials. He had seen sailors who died of violence dropped overboard with no more ceremony than if they had been so many stones. How different this Christian funeral! His soul cried out that it was heaven even to die in this Christian land.

Then there occurred one of those unusual manifestations which so often proved that Samuel Morris possessed the superhuman power conferred only by God's own Spirit. As the service went on, man after man came forward, without spoken invitation,

and kneeled beside the casket. They came
not as mourners of the dead but as penitents
from the "body of death" which is sin,
drawn by the divine Light that radiated
from the soul of Samuel Morris.

Sammy Goes to College

After the funeral, Merritt took Sammy
with him in the coach to his office. On the
way Sammy asked so many searching
questions about the Holy Ghost that Merritt
soon discovered that he was the one taught
rather than the teacher; that Samuel Morris' religious experience exceeded his own
studied knowledge of God's invisible Messenger. At the office Merritt dictated a letter to the president of Taylor University,
then located in Ft. Wayne, Indiana. He said
that he was sending to them a diamond in
the rough for them to polish and to send
out to enlighten the world.

The next day was Sunday. Mr. Merritt
said to Sammy, "I would like you to ac-
company me to Sunday School today. I am
the superintendent and may ask you to
speak."

Sammy answered, "I never was in a
Sunday School, but all right!"

Stephen Merritt smilingly introduced
him as one, Samuel Morris, who had come
from Africa to talk to their superintendent

about the Holy Ghost. The school laughed. After this introduction, Merritt was called from the platform to attend to another matter. A moment later when he returned— lo! the altar was full of young people, weeping and sobbing. Sammy was standing by the railing, praying.

Sammy himself was perfectly calm. He was unusually quiet by nature. When he prayed he always used the same matter-of-fact tone that one would use in speaking to a human friend. He just "talked to his Father"—earnestly but calmly. His audience was not swayed by any of the oratorical tricks of the professional revivalist. It was not his exact words or manner that seemed to matter, but the presence of the power of the Holy Ghost was so clearly felt that the entire place was filled with His glory.

These young people of the Sunday School organized spontaneously and immediately a Samuel Morris Missionary Society. This Society hurriedly secured money for carfare, additional clothing, and everything necessary to send Samuel Morris to school. They filled three trunks with books, clothing and other gifts.

After the Sunday School service Sammy returned to the Merritts' residence. Out of politeness Mrs. Merritt asked him to return thanks at table. His heart was filled with thanksgiving. His expressions of gratitude to his heavenly Father melted all hearts. Even Mrs. Merritt who was unemotional and schooled in an aristocratic reserve could not but weep. She said to Sammy, "Make this your home. Whatever we have we will share with you." His brief stay had removed all trace of race prejudice in that home.

However, it had been decided that Sammy should have an education. By the middle of the week he was ready to take the train to Ft. Wayne. Samuel Morris reached that town on Friday, his Deliverance Day, his day of fasting and prayer. At the time of his arrival he was little better off than he had been when he descended from the ship as a stranger in a strange land. He had some books which he could not read, some clothing, and a few gifts of nominal value. To all he seemed just a poor, black boy whose preparatory training had been sadly neglected.

Nevertheless, this young man soon revealed a spirit all too rare among Christians. When President Thaddeus C. Reade asked him what room he wanted, Sammy replied, "If there is a room nobody wants, give that to me." Of this incident Dr. Reade later wrote: "I turned away for my eyes were full of tears. I was asking myself whether I was willing to take what nobody else wanted. In my experience as a teacher, I have had occasion to assign rooms to more than a thousand students. Most of them were noble, Christian young ladies and gentlemen, but Sammy Morris was the only one of them who ever said, 'If there is a room that nobody wants, give that to me.' "

However, when President Reade enrolled him, it was with a heavy heart. He could see no talent in this unattractive black boy; he could see only another weight added to the financial burden which was already too great to be borne. Taylor University was then on the verge of closing its doors because of a shortage of funds and even of food for the students. Involuntary fasting was much in evidence. Dr. Reade, always a man of action, battled daily to keep the wolf from the door. On Saturday he was out of the city on business. Sunday he had an appointment to preach in the Methodist Church in Churubusco, a very small church with a poor congregation.

Dr. Reade made a strong appeal for aid. He told them about the Negro boy who had arrived on Friday from Africa without a dollar to his name; how he had accepted him as a student in the faith that some would come forward to help support and educate him. The financial response to Dr. Reade's appeal was discouraging in the extreme. It was almost a flat failure. A Mr.

Thomas handed him fifty cents. But that was all.

As Dr. Reade was leaving the next day, a butcher by the name of Josiah Kichler, a poor man and not a member of the church, called to him. Mr. Kichler said, "Doctor, I heard your appeal for help for that poor black boy from Africa. The Spirit tells me to give this to your Faith Fund." He handed Dr. Reade a five dollar bill.

But he gave Dr. Reade something even more valuable. That five dollar bill gave him a new idea that pierced the gloom hanging over Taylor University. He appropriated Mr. Kichler's phrase, and started the Samuel Morris "Faith Fund" with that five dollar bill. It shall be a memorial to Josiah Kichler as long as Samuel Morris' name is known and revered.

Other donors soon began to contribute to this Fund. When Sammy was informed of the increasing amounts coming in for him, he said to Dr. Reade: "No, that money is not mine. That is God's money. I want you to use it for others more worthy than I." Samuel Morris never put a penny of this Fund in his own pocket. He never bought anything for himself. Dr. Reade paid for his meagre necessities. He would accept nothing else.

At one time he even came to Dr. Reade and asked him if he could leave the school

for a while to go out and earn money. Dr.
Reade was taken by surprise. Sammy explained: "I do not want to leave school. But
I want to earn money enough to bring Henry
O'Neil over here to be educated. He is a
much better boy than I. He worked with
me for Jesus in Liberia."

Dr. Reade told Sammy to pray over it
and a way would be provided to bring Henry
O'Neil to America. Next morning, Sammy
all smiles came to Dr. Reade, saying,
"Henry O'Neil is coming over soon. My
Father has just told me."

Dr. Reade wrote Stephen Merritt about
it, and found that one of the missionaries
who had been in Liberia when Sammy and
Henry were doing such valuable work had
returned to St. Louis and was arranging at
that very time to have Henry O'Neil
brought over and educated. He was brought
from Africa—the first fruits of Samuel Morris' own ministry.

PART III.
THE STUDENT LEADER

A Minister Ordained by Heaven

The Apostle Paul often affirmed that, unlike the other apostles, his license to preach came not from men but directly from heaven. That was true of Samuel Morris.

On the Sunday following his arrival in Ft. Wayne, Sammy asked if there were a Negro church in Ft. Wayne, and was told that there was. He started out to find it, but it was so far from the college building that he was late in reaching it. The preliminaries of the service were all over. The minister was in the pulpit, had announced his text, and was ready to preach. Sammy walked straight down through the church to the platform and went up a step or two toward the pulpit.

The minister was a very strict disciplinarian and set in his ways. Sammy's boldness was very disconcerting to him. Sammy said, "I am Samuel Morris. I just came from Africa. I have a message for your people." The minister's first impulse was to refuse him, but when he looked into Sammy's radiant face and flashing eyes, he sensed that there might be a message. He asked Sammy if he had his sermon prepared, thinking he was an ordained minister. Sammy said, "No, but I have a message."

Sammy was given the pulpit. The pastor had hardly sat down by the collection table when he heard a commotion and looked up to see the whole body of the congregation on their knees, weeping, praying, and shouting for joy. Sammy was in the pulpit, not preaching, but praying—"talking to his Father." Afterward the minister said of this occasion, "I did not listen to hear what he was saying. I was seized with an overpowering desire to pray. What I said and what Sammy said I do not remember, but I know my soul was on fire as never before. The light that had brought Samuel Morris out of bondage in Africa was surely shining into the hearts of our brethren there in Ft. Wayne. No such visitation of the Holy Spirit had ever been witnessed by that congregation."

The meeting lasted long after the allotted time. When the people finally left for their homes, they carried with them the realization of a living revelation of the Holy Ghost. Samuel Morris had spoken the language of the human soul. He had appealed to their heavenly Father from the depths of his own soul. His intercession had been uttered in absolute faith, and the Spirit was there in answer to that childlike faith. They all went home rejoicing.

In a single day, the unknown Samuel Morris had become a name to reckon with in Ft. Wayne. The local newspapers ran editorials about Samuel Morris' great revival that Sunday at the African M. E. Church on East Wayne Street. Religious papers far and wide copied and commented upon this wonderful spiritual manifestation. All Ft. Wayne knew about the new African student at Taylor University before he had been there a week.

However, the education of Samuel Morris presented a serious problem. He could not enter any of the regular classes. He would require several years of continuous training before he could be enrolled as a college student. He was about eighteen years of age, but in book learning he was like a child of seven or eight years. The only solution was to arrange for a long period of private instruction through tutors. At chapel, Dr. Reade explained Sammy's difficulty, and called for volunteers to teach this black boy. It would be no light task. Miss Harriet Stemen, daughter of Dr. Christian B. Stemen, a Christian physician, and Dr. Reade's own daughter, both volunteered as tutors and were duly assigned to the work. Others, including Dr. Idora Rose and Miss Grace Husted, subsequently assisted Sammy at various times with his lessons. But Harriet Stemen assumed the chief responsibility for his educational progress.

Sammy Saves a University

Samuel Morris was a diligent student. Every word, every thought, every principle, taught him was indelibly fixed in his mind. The refined expressions and the musical accents of his teachers' voices were transferred to his own conversation. Yet he remained original in his thinking. His grouping of words into sentences was a wonder to all. His sentences were short, but every word in them had meaning. Idle talk was unknown to him. High ideals and noble purposes were his very existence. Miss Stemen and Miss Reade soon learned that the burden they had volunteered to carry was to become a well-rewarded labor of love. Every day brought new blessings to his consecrated teachers.

But Samuel continued to regard the divine Spirit of Truth as his chief instructor. Often in solving a difficult arithmetical problem, he would say in low, audible tones, "Lord, help!" He spent more time "talking to his Father" than he did with any earthly teachers. The Holy Spirit brought God as close to him as any earthly teacher could be, and made Him equally real.

Many came from a distance to see Samuel Morris and to talk to him, but he had

no time for mere gossip. After the custom-
ary greeting Sammy would hand the visitor
the Bible, opened at the chapter he wished
to study, and would ask him to read aloud.
Sammy undertook to have the entire Bible
read to him in this way.

There was a young man in the University
who was an atheist of the aggressive type.
He was not satisfied to let others believe
as they pleased. He was well versed in all
the stock arguments of the atheistic cult,
and never lost an opportunity to engage in
an argument with believing students. It was
not always easy to get an immediate audience with Sammy. He would not admit anyone when he was engaged in prayer. However, this atheist prevailed upon some of
the students to take him to Sammy's room
and introduce him. The atheist was all
wound up for an argument, and expected
an easy victory over the unlettered Negro.
As usual Sammy handed him the open Bible
and asked him to read a chapter. The atheist threw the Bible on the table, and said,
"I do not read that book any more. It is
full of love affairs, wars, and a lot of big
'fish stories.' I don't believe a word of it."

Sammy had never talked with an atheist
before; even the African pagans believe in
a deity. He sat still and eyed the atheist
until he had run down. Then Sammy arose
to his feet and said, "My dear brother, your

Father speaks to you and you do not believe Him? Your Brother speaks, and you do not believe Him? The Sun shines and you do not believe it? God is your Father; Christ your Brother; the Holy Ghost your Sun."

Then, putting his hand on his visitor's shoulder he said: "Kneel down, and I will pray for you." A soul was at stake; the divine Spirit taught him how to speak in the language of this brother's heart. He touched the tenderest cords. The atheist resisted until he was leaving the room when he felt the dart of the convicting Spirit in his heart. At the end of that term, he left the university a praying, working Christian. Later, this one-time scoffer became a bishop!

The leadership of Samuel Morris was no less felt by the majority of the student body than by the exceptional skeptics among them. While most of the students were sincere Christians, this was a period in which there was a weakening of faith and a growing worldliness among churches and church colleges. The Darwinian theory of evolution then seemed to strike at the foundation of Biblical authority. The increase of wealth through scientific inventions fostered materialism. They could not then foresee the present day of economic depressions, worldwide wars, and totalitarian philosophies which have demonstrated that impersonal science falls far short of being a substitute for a personal religion.

Taylor University was then controlled by a ministerial association of the Methodist Episcopal Church, and maintained an unusually high spiritual standard of education. Yet, already a vast majority of the laymen and some clergymen of that denomination had ceased to have more than a nominal faith in the advanced work of the Holy Spirit as experienced and proclaimed by the founder of Methodism. John Wesley had taught that the state of pure love and holiness so often enjoined by the Scriptures can actually be maintained by the cleansing power of the Holy Spirit. Such a blameless life was not free from temptation or the power to sin. But, the sanctified believer was given the power not to sin because his will had been liberated from the power of inbred evil and its hindering or over-mastering temptations.

Regardless of disputes over this doctrine of sanctification, it is certain that the key to Wesley's own amazing power of leadership was found in his boldness of faith in the miraculous power of God's Spirit. In fact, the dynamic of all successful evangelism is found in the power of a Spirit-filled life. But this kind of faith and power had begun to wane at Taylor as elsewhere.

Samuel Morris electrified the entire university from the president down to the newest freshman by demonstrating the simplicity and power with which the Holy Spirit can confer all the graces of leadership upon the humblest human being. The whole school was lifted to a higher plane in which the students were not merely "saved," but spiritually strengthened to save others.

The Spirit of God is the guarantor of material as well as spiritual blessings. The spiritual leadership of Samuel Morris, who sought first the Kingdom of Heaven, did not fail to bring to Taylor University "all these other things," as added blessings. It was during his student days that the university came to the end of its financial resources, and the board of trustees held what appeared to be their last meeting. It was the inspiration of Samuel Morris that came to the rescue.

The Samuel Morris Faith Fund took the present writer to the university at the time when the trustees were singing their swan song. It seemed that no school with such an asset as Samuel Morris could perish. I believed that his fund would bring in enough cash to tide us over, and I expressed that conviction. The late Colonel D. N. Foster, then president of the Board, said, "But what can we do now? Where can we go? We must move from here soon."

I replied, "Come to Upland. We will receive you with open arms."

They consulted together and then said,
"We would need ten thousand dollars and
ten acres of land."

With the infection of Sammy's own faith,
I replied, "Gentlemen, you will go to Upland. I have no authority to enter into a
contract with you to that effect, but tomor-
row I will go to Upland and telegraph you
to come there and get your ten thousand
dollars and select your ten acres of land."

Samuel Morris held my overcoat for me
that morning when I was getting ready
to go to the train. To me he was the Moses
that would lead Taylor out of the wilderness
into the land of promise. I arrived in Upland
about ten o'clock. By two o'clock the ten
thousand dollars had been raised, and
enough more to buy the ten acres of land.
Samuel Morris and Taylor University were
on every tongue in Upland. A committee
was appointed to go at once to Ft. Wayne
to negotiate a contract with the trustees.
The Committee visited Sammy and were
as much impressed by him as were we
who had known him longer. The contract
was signed, and the beautiful site of the
present campus was selected.

The Last Adventure

There was nothing abnormal about the
mysticism of Samuel Morris. Child of the

wilderness, he remained a lover of nature. He found God not only in the Spirit within his breast but also in the external beauty reflecting the handiwork of the Creator.

He often compared the beauty of America with that of his homeland. In Africa they had beautiful flowers but without perfume. He loved to take long walks in our woods, inhaling the odor of our wild flowers and listening to the enchanting songs of the robins, meadow-larks, and mocking birds. When fall began to tint the leaves of the trees with many hues and colors, Sammy, accustomed only to the green of the tropics, beheld them with an ecstasy of joy. He would fairly shout his thanks to his heavenly Father that his eyes had seen such wonders. He would often say, "God is surely good to you folks in Indiana."

On Thanksgiving evening, after the usual dinner, Sammy was asked by Dr. Reade which country—Africa or America—he liked best. He laughed and replied: "Which is better, roast turkey or raw monkey?" "Why, Sammy," Dr. Reade said, "you did not eat monkeys?" "O yes, sir," he answered, "I ate many monkeys and ate them raw!" Yet it was to his own land that he yearned to return in order to share his new-found blessings with those of his own kind and color.

One time when he hurt the back of his

hand so that the outer skin was removed, he put ink on the lighter tissue exposed. He explained to his teacher that he was afraid that it would turn white, and be a disgrace and hindrance to him when he returned to Africa to preach. Because he was God's child, he was never ashamed of his color.

The first snow that fell after Sammy came to Ft. Wayne happened to be of the large, flaky kind. It began in the night and was still falling when Sammy awoke in the morning. When he looked out of the window and saw everything covered with a sparkling white blanket, his surprise and awe knew no bounds. There was no word in his language for snow, for it was unknown in his native region. He had never seen or even heard of it. He rushed out into the snow and gathered up a handful, saying, "These must be messages from Heaven to us. If I could only read them, what a wonderful story they would tell us! Earth has nothing half so beautiful. God alone has such a pattern."

As he spoke, his warm hand melted the snow in it. He said to Dr. Reade, "Where did it go? It has left only a few drops of water!" His black face was a picture of adoration. His eyes filled with tears. He raised his hand, and prayed to his Father to teach him and all about him how to read these beautiful messages from Heaven. As he finished his prayer he said, "A year here is worth a lifetime in Africa."

That winter an evangelist conducted a series of joint revival services in the old roller skating rink on West Main Street. A great throng attended nightly. Samuel Morris especially enjoyed the singing. His very soul seemed set to music. When the congregation sang, his voice could be heard in every corner of the big building.

He was always given a place on the platform. If the floor workers encountered a stubborn response, a sign from one of them would catch Sammy's eye. In a short time there would be two on their knees, or Sammy would return bringing a penitent to the altar. No one hesitated or refused his invitation to kneel and pray. High hats and silk gowns were no bar. His race and color did not offend, for all recognized his spiritual power and grace. He did little exhorting that winter but much singing and praying.

The tortures Sammy had endured in Africa while serving as a pawn and the severe hardships he had suffered aboard the tramp ship had greatly weakened his frail constitution. Our rigorous northern climate with its long, cold winters was an unnatural environment for one reared in the tropics. Nevertheless, Samuel Morris continued to be a regular attendant at religious meetings during the exceptionally severe winter of 1892-93.

He caught a severe cold in the month of January while attending the Berry Street Methodist Church. He kept silent about it and bore his illness as if nothing were amiss. It did not matter to him that the night was dark and stormy with a temperature of twenty degrees below zero. He felt it was his duty as well as pleasure to be there. His honest, black face and his simple, steadfast faith were an inspiration to the minister to give his best to his congregation.

Samuel Morris sacrificed his health to the service of God. The very last meeting at the church was attended by him. Some still remember how he stepped forward just before the benediction and led the congregation in one of the tender anthems beloved by millions of Christians, "The Old, Old Story . . . of Jesus and His Love."

Though Sammy lacked the resistance to shake off the cold he had contracted, he continued to attend his classes as usual. But his strength waned. He developed the symptoms of dropsy and could no longer hide the fact that he was gravely ill. When Dr. Stemen observed his condition, he was taken to the St. Joseph Hospital. Had he been the president's own son, he could not have had kinder and better care. Many

who had learned to love him and whose
souls he had blessed came to visit him.
They brought him tokens of their affection.
Love he gave, and love he received beyond
measure.

At first Sammy could not comprehend
why he should be ill. He said, "When I
froze my ears last winter, they hurt me
very much. I asked my Father about it,
and they quit hurting me right away. Now,
I cannot get well. I cannot understand it."

But one day when the students came
to pay him their daily visit, Sammy told
them with quiet joy that he now understood
it all. He said: "I am so happy. I have
seen the angels. They are coming for me
soon. The light my Father in heaven sent
to save me when I was hanging helpless
on that cross in Africa was for a purpose.
I was saved for a purpose. Now I have
fulfilled that purpose. My work here on
earth has been finished."

Dr. Reade questioned him about the
great work he had planned to do among
his own people in Africa. Sammy answered, "It is not 'my work.' It is Christ's
work. He must choose His own workers.
Others can do it better."

Dr. Stemen lived directly across the
street from the hospital. In the forenoon
of May 12, Dr. Stemen was mowing his
lawn. He heard a voice calling, "Don't work

too hard, Dr. Stemen." He glanced up and
saw Sammy looking out of the window of
his hospital room. They waved greetings.
Sammy left the window and reclined once
more in his chair. Dr. Stemen returned
to his work.

A few minutes later Sister Helen of the
hospital came down and notified Dr. Stemen and his family that Sammy seemed
helpless. When Dr. Stemen reached him,
the young African was sitting peacefully
in his chair. He was dead.

His face wore an expression of solemn
joy like that with which he had often intoned
his favorite hymn—

> Fade, fade, each earthly joy,
> Jesus is mine,
> Break every tender tie,
> Jesus is mine!
> Dark is the wilderness,
> Earth has no resting place,
> Jesus alone can bless.
> Jesus is mine!

He had gone to meet his heavenly Father
as calmly as he would have greeted one
of his beloved teachers. The "angel in ebony" had joined the angels of all the ages
and all the races.

A Passing Cloud of Doubt

Taylor University had been preparing

for the laying of the cornerstone of its new home in Upland. The railroads were preparing to run excursion trains for the event. Samuel Morris was to have spoken and sung. He was counted upon as the principal attraction, although a bishop and other notables were to participate. The passing of Samuel Morris plunged the entire community into profound grief. God seemed no longer near at hand. In every heart was dumb wonderment at the mystery of Divine Providence in taking away a life so young and of such glorious promise of usefulness. Was all his faith to end in a cloud of doubt?

The body of Samuel Morris lay in state in the college chapel until the funeral services. The student body carried his casket many blocks to the Berry Street Methodist Church of which he was a member. Hundreds stood along the street with bared heads, and other hundreds were unable to enter the crowded church.

After the services the burial ceremony in Lindenwood Cemetery, his last earthly resting place, was attended by a multitude such as had never before accompanied a funeral there. Miss Stemen, his teacher, contributed his first tombstone.

The senior class of Taylor University in 1928 sponsored the erection of the present monument upon a hill that in spring and summer smiles with nature's choicest blossoms. The stone bears the inscription:

SAMUEL MORRIS, 1872-1893
Prince Kaboo
Native of West Africa
* * *
Famous Christian Mystic
Apostle of Simple Faith
Exponent of the Spirit-filled Life

After the first shock of grief and consternation had passed, the real significance of the life and mission of Samuel Morris began to dawn upon the minds of his teachers, students, and friends. God's purpose and plan for Sammy had been wiser and grander than theirs. Dr. Reade voiced this truth when he wrote: "Samuel Morris was a divinely sent messenger of God to Taylor University. He thought he was coming over here to prepare himself for his mission to his people, but his coming was to prepare Taylor University for her mission to the whole world. Taylor got a vision of the world's need through him. It was no longer local, it was worldwide."

Faith Finds a Better Way

The cloud of doubt quickly lifted as evidence began to mount that Sammy's faith had found a better way. His March of Faith had only begun! He had desired, above all, to bring the message of Christian salvation and of the power of the Holy Spirit, to his own people in Africa. But had Samuel Morris himself lived to return to Africa, his personal influence would have been limited to some one small region of that vast continent. His departure from this life led immediately to a manifold increase and spread of missionary effort.

At the first prayer meeting held after Sammy's death, a young man arose and said: "I feel impressed this moment that I must go to Africa in Sammy's place; and I pray that as his work has fallen upon me so the mantle of his faith may likewise fall upon me." He was at once followed by two other volunteers for the African field. And these were but the vanguard of still more to follow.

Moreover, death only served to extend the influence of Samuel Morris in another way. Had Sammy himself returned to Africa, he would have become identified wholly with the Negro race. It is natural and proper that his own people should find a special inspiration in his life and example. But his early death while living as a student in a school where he was the only black person has identified him with Caucasian as well as Negro. Consequently, the message of his potent faith has become a blessing to men of every race and color.

More than that, it has served to create a bond of understanding between the two races. His very burial ground typifies this unique bond of Christian brotherhood between white and black people. His grave has been removed to a beautiful plot midway between the respective sections reserved for the two races. White people as well as black come to visit the tomb of Samuel Morris in greater numbers than that of any other person, though thousands of good and noble individuals lie buried there. Thus, he serves his own race all the more effectively by overcoming racial prejudice.

PART IV.

Key to Democratic Leadership

There are other moral gains in the early death of Samuel Morris. Never having reached maturity, he has become like the dark youth upon Keat's Grecian urn, "Forever young, forever fair."

He will always typify the preparatory life of the college student rather than that of the mature world. He appeals, therefore, to present-day students more strongly than any adult. For the student world of today his life and, even more truly, his death point the way to the most successful form of leadership in a democracy.

He never reached the age of twenty-one; and he lived but a scant five years after coming out of the jungle. Yet in that short time, about equivalent to high school years, he made a name known around the world. His life story has been translated into five languages. Few religious leaders, if any, are more widely influential with missionaries of all the various church denominations.

Yet all this touches only the fringe of the essential greatness of his leadership. The greatest leaders are not those who win the most followers. Such leaders are often dangerous to democratic institutions. They tend to become mob leaders, demagogues, and dictators. The greatest leadership is that which creates other leaders. Democracy depends for its preservation upon the capacity to pass on the torch of leadership from one generation to another—the March of Faith through the ages.

The truly democratic leader has the humility and fraternity which encourage others to assert their powers and to strengthen and replace him when he is gone. This is the kind of leadership America sorely needs. Samuel Morris affords a shining example of this democratic leadership. A single illustration will show how his influence created the same powers of leadership in others. How Sammy converted an aggressive atheist to Christianity has already been told. Now comes the sequel.

After this same atheist had become a preacher, he met one of his old atheistic friends who was just as aggressive as he himself had once been. There was a clashing of minds at once, and the argument waxed warm. The preacher said something that angered his antagonist so much that he dealt the minister a blow. It felled him to the ground unconscious. When he became conscious he was filled with wrath.

His antagonist was standing over him exultingly. Suddenly, the minister thought of Samuel Morris when he was lying on the cabin floor of the tramp ship, felled by a blow of the captain's fist. He said to himself: "If Samuel Morris could forgive that cruel captain and save him, why can't I do the same for this man?" His anger left him; he got to his knees and began praying for his enemy. As he prayed, the atheist knelt down by his side, put his arm around him, wiped from his face the blood that was still flowing, and begged his forgiveness. Soon he was crying to the Lord for forgiveness of his sins. His surrender was complete. The bishop baptized him; and he became an active leader in church work.

Thus, Samuel Morris had created another leader endowed with all his own charity and spiritual power; and he, in turn, had communicated the same Christian spirit to yet another soul who became a leader also. Our country needs more unselfish leaders who can literally multiply their own efficiency in this way, and who can also project their plans securely even beyond their own lifetimes.

Cure for Inferiority Complex

Samuel Morris brings to every modern youth the strongest encouragement to develop his or her powers of leadership, no matter what may be the handicaps of race, color, poverty. Better than any other person of modern times the life of Morris proves that the invisible Spirit of God can make the most unlikely person a leader of power and charm. This is true of every young man and woman, regardless of his present inferiority complex.

Let us try to find one merely human attribute of Samuel Morris that could explain his instant and profound influence over the souls of others of every rank and kind.

He belonged to the Negro race which is the object of such adverse prejudice.

He was short of stature and unimpressive in appearance.

He had not a penny of wealth.

He was unlettered and ignorant. Though his pronunciation was good, he had no oratorical command of the English language whereby he might sway an audience with the magic of words.

In an age of literary propaganda, he wrote nothing to disseminate and perpetuate his ideas.

No organization backed him. He was without even family supporters, being a fugitive from his own home and people.

Surely, there is nothing in this inventory

of human qualities to make a great leader of souls. Yet this penniless and homeless waif was able to make all heads bow before him, whether they were those of brutal seamen or bishops of the church, natives of the wilderness or professors of the university. Only God could perform that miracle!

Yet, it not only is the privilege but also the duty of every Christian youth to possess and exercise that same divine dynamic. In that truth lies the open sesame to effective leadership for every youth who will extend the hand of faith to accept this gift of the Holy Spirit.

Scientific Proof of Divinity

Finally, the example of Samuel Morris not only encourages every youth to aspire to dynamic leadership, but also makes easy the necessary faith in God by furnishing a scientific proof of divinity. In this scientific age the student world rightly demands the evidence of facts in support of its beliefs. True religion does not rest upon blind faith but upon a reasoned faith supported by evidences as tangible, logical, historical, and experimental as those supporting any modern science.

While Samuel Morris was yet alive it would have been difficult, indeed, to rationalize the known facts of his leadership by

any other theory than that of divine endow-
ment because his personality was otherwise
so unattractive and so handicapped. But
it is his early death that has made the
scientific experiment "airtight."

So long as he was alive, the "last ditch"
doubter could always entertain the far-
fetched notion that some unknown kind of
"animal magnetism" or some merely human emotional force of his personality ac-
counted for the reactions of those influenced
by the "angel in ebony." For that matter,
scientists have given up the idea of absolute
proof so long as they are dealing with a
physical object. A test tube in the chemical
laboratory may always contain some unknown or microscopic element that creates
doubt as to the result of the test.

But that other dark angel, Death, has
ended all possibility of error due to the
influence of physical magnetism, emotional
contagion, or any other mortal cause. The
entire human personality ends with death
and burial.

Yet, the leadership of Samuel Morris
did not change its character or lose its
force with his death. The divine element
in his Spirit-filled personality—the ever-
living Spirit of God—has continued to carry
on his work and ministry with undiminished
force. Herein is proof positive of the divinity
animating his spirit during life, a proof

even more conclusive than that of the chemical laboratory, regardless of its checking and rechecking of any physical tests.

Napoleon confessed that Jesus Christ was a greater leader than himself because he could command the loyalty of his army only so long as he was alive and present; but the army of Christ's followers remains loyal and continues to grow centuries after the death of their Captain. Only a divine Saviour can survive a Cross; and only a divinely led follower of Christ can continue to bear increasing fruit long after his physical presence and human powers are no more. Samuel Morris meets this acid test. The passing of the physical body of Samuel Morris has but served to perpetuate and magnify the work of the Holy Spirit with whom he walked so closely.

"He Being Dead Yet Speaketh"

It is not in isolated instances that we find scientific evidence of the continuing leadership of Samuel Morris through the operation of the Holy Spirit. Everywhere his contacts have proved fruitful long years after his human powers have ceased.

Following the sudden death of Sammy, it will be recalled, only three students at Taylor University volunteered to take his place as a missionary to Africa. This might be set down by the skeptic to mere emotional reaction from his death. But his influence has been producing the very same results in increasing volume for decades. Seven students—more than twice as many —went out from this same school to Africa in one recent year alone. These seven were as truly the result of Sammy's spiritual leadership as were the earlier three, because Taylor University before his advent was an ordinary college without a special missionary vision and purpose.

And these seven later fruits of his leadership are but a handful of the unending results of his divinely inspired and empowered leadership. Many in other years were prompted by his influence to go forth as Christian teachers and preachers to Africa. Several notable missionaries from Taylor have made the supreme sacrifice and are now buried in African soil—Oliver Moody, Susan Talbot Wengatz, and John C. Ovenshire. There is a Taylor University Bible School in Africa.

And this is but a small segment of his ever-widening and deepening influence more than a generation after his departure from this life! Taylor University has become a training ground for missionaries and Christian teachers going out to all the four corners of the earth—a greater evangelization work than even Samuel Morris envisaged during his physical lifetime.

But there is even more conclusive proof of the divine element in his life. Much of his continued leadership has been manifested entirely without the support or intervention of any human agency or literature. For example, the new spirit which Sammy infused into the ship's crew of rough seamen during his voyage to America was no transitory change. Several years after Samuel Morris came to New York on the tramp ship, the old captain returned to New York and sought out Stephen Merritt. When Merritt told him that Samuel Morris had gone to glory before he was twenty-one years old, the old captain was so overcome that he could not talk for some time.

He stated that most of the old crew were still with him, and were anxiously awaiting his return for word from their hero and minister. He said that Sammy had offered the first audible prayer ever heard aboard his ship. He testified to the wonderful influence Sammy exercised over such a motley crew of hardened men. That crew had become like one family. Sammy's teachings had wrought lasting benefits.

Upon Rev. Stephen Merritt himself the influence of the Negro boy who could scarcely speak English proved to be lifelong. Sammy had spent only a week with him in New York; yet the strong faith of the "angel in ebony" continued to work miracles as long as Merritt lived. After Sammy's departure, Merritt went to the hospitals for the insane and prayed for them, and many were restored to reason; he visited hospitals for the ill and prayed for them, and many were healed. Before the end of Stephen Merritt's pastorate ten thousand persons had been brought to the Cross.

The effect of Sammy's brief appearance at the Jane Street Sunday School was enduring. For many years the missionary group formed spontaneously at the time of his visit continued to be a power for good. The following winter more than a thousand new members were added. The beneficent influence of Samuel Morris was extended to a legion of needy souls through this one society.

The African M. E. Church which Sammy had visited in Ft. Wayne had not experienced a mere gust of emotional excitement when he prayed in their pulpit. The spiritual strength conferred at that time wrought a lasting change. More members were added to the church during the following winter than ever before. Eventually, they were able to build for themselves a new brick church.

The Samuel Morris Faith Fund continued to operate and to serve its unselfish

purpose long after the decease of Samuel
Morris. Three years later it was aiding
in the support of one hundred needy students preparing for missionary work. Do-
nations at first came from various parts
of the country; then, from foreign lands.
Over twenty thousand dollars came in within a short time. Today, after the lapse of
more than forty-five years, unsolicited con-
tributions are still received to that Fund.

It is difficult to imagine any American
University for white students naming one
of its permanent college buildings in honor
of a penniless Negro. Yet this was done
at Taylor University. Such, has been the
lasting influence of Samuel Morris that one
acccepts the Samuel Morris Faith Memorial
Hall of today as a natural and inevitable
feature of the campus.

Nor was this enduring honor a mere
manifestation of the campus spirit. The entire city of Fort Wayne, speaking through
its Civic League, has just recommended
that a new housing project of that city,
under general authority of the United States
Housing Authority, shall be known as
Samuel Morris Village. Thus, the benign
influence of Sammy will continue to prove
an inspiration and a blessing to the under-
privileged for years to come.

Even his burial place, though a symbol
of death, is today a shrine at which the

Holy Spirit actively carries on the life mission of Samuel Morris. The grave is now the scene of religious meetings, large and small, and of unusual conversions. For instance, a woman who had lost her health, her husband, and her savings, was unable to find work. At her wit's end she had gathered wildflowers for her husband's tomb, and sank down on the ground in a state of complete collapse longing only for death.

Then, something led her to follow a group visiting the nearby grave of Samuel Morris. She thought, "If the Lord could save him when he had nothing, he can save me." She prayed. She seemed to hear Sammy's voice saying, "Pray to my Father; He will save you. He will send the Holy Ghost to lead you." She felt the presence of the Spirit of God. Her prayers were answered!

She joined the Salvation Army. Since that time, when she has had an especially hardened and cynical person to deal with, she has brought him to the same sacred spot for prayers. In not one instance has there been a failure of saving grace. The same benediction of God has been felt at Sammy's grave by thousands of others who have been converted there or endowed with a fresh measure of spiritual vision and strength.

Today, thanks to the enduring influence of his Spirit-powered life, millions of laymen have felt, and millions more will feel, the vitalizing challenge of this undying faith. Such successful living, and yet more successful dying, foreshadows that immortality proclaimed by Jesus: "Whosoever shall lose his life for my sake shall find it." We can only conclude with the thought affirmed by Doctor Reade in all simplicity: "He is not dead!" Like the soul of John Brown, the unconquerable and conquering spirit of Samuel Morris goes marching on!

Churches may close their doors. Creeds may pass away. Ethics may change. But the simple faith of this adventurous spirit was stayed on none of these. He brought men face to face once more with the living Christ whom to know is to love and follow. This is the secret of the leadership that has no end. In this secret strength America will yet go forward in her March of Faith.

EPILOGUE

"Greater Works Than These"

A wonderful coincidence has recently furnished proof of the most amazing of all the miracles recorded in the foregoing pages. Many readers, including Christians, wrongly suppose that the age of miracles is past. They do not understand that the divine Messenger, the Holy Spirit, is not afar off but daily at work here on earth guiding the destinies of men and nations.

No doubt, the miracle that is hardest to believe in the life of Samuel Morris is that of the mysterious light which dazzled the captors of Kaboo, and then guided him at night through the forest to safety. All previous biographers have suppressed this marvel of divine grace, fearing the incredulity of their readers or lacking an orthodox explanation.

But, an exactly parallel case is now on record, attested by an unimpeachable witness, F. R. Burroughs, missionary to China. A Chinese youth named Ging-Hua, like Kaboo, was his father's eldest son, and was similarly carried off and held for ransom by a band of men who were in the habit of torturing their captives in order to extract ransom money from their families. Ging-Hua was lying bound with ropes and surrounded by his captors when, suddenly, a golden light shone around him, and he recognized that it was of heavenly origin. By its illumination he was enabled to untie his ropes and to escape from the camp.

But where was he? He knew not what direction to take. It was dark, and his captors had taken him far from home by unfrequented paths. Then the kindly light formed itself into a long beam, pointing from heaven right on the path ahead. The light led him, step by step, straight to his family and safety. Thus, the miraculous rescue of Kaboo has been duplicated in every essential feature.

To the skeptic I suggest that the very reason why both physical and spiritual miracles seem out of place nowadays is that our generation lacks the absolute and unquestioning faith of a Morris which was the necessary condition of the divine promise of "greater works" to follow the advent of the Holy Spirit. "Most of us," wrote Dr. Reade, "have gone too far away from the simple faith of childhood and God cannot do many mighty works in us because of our unbelief."

Fortunately, there are always a few valiant believers to refute the notion that God no longer performs wonders on earth. An incident of this kind occurred in con-

nection with the present book. The first
draft of my manuscript was read to Dr.
Harriet Stemen MacBeth, Sammy's teacher, some time ago. That reading was followed by one of those endless miracles of
grace that still attend the footsteps of Samuel Morris. Though bedridden for weeks
and nearly blind, she immediately arose,
restored to health and strength.

To the Leaders of Tomorrow

Whatever may be thought of the other
miracles in this book, the central miracle
in the life of Samuel Morris is one that
can be reproduced in the life of every read-
er. You do not need to be hanging over
a cross-tree in Africa to have the light of
Heaven flood your soul, empowering you
for God's service. You need only to come
face to face with your own personal help-
lessness without God, and to acknowledge
His grace and power.

Never was it easier to make such a con-
fession of man's need of God than now
when the power of evil triumphs over whole
nations; the failure of all man-made reme-
dies for world ills leaves no choice but a
transforming change in the nature of man
himself.

The triumphant leadership of Samuel
Morris affords an inspiring example to both

young and old. However, his youth, coura-
geous faith and undying works qualify this
biography especially as a guide to the youth
who are now preparing to take leading roles
in American life.

Of course, all our youth will not become
ministers and missionaries specializing in
religious work. But one of the most remarkable features of the life of Samuel Morris
is that all his amazing spiritual influence
was exercised as an incident to ordinary
secular occupations. He found time and
opportunity to bring the richest blessings
of God to his associates while he was toil-
ing long hours as a plantation worker, a
house painter, and a cabin boy, and, later,
while he was studying overtime as a college
student trying to catch up with fellow students more favored with leisure. Any youth
has an equal opportunity to serve God in
his daily contacts.

Moreover, he put the same religious zeal
into his workaday tasks, such as cleaning
the captain's cabin, that he did in his verbal
preachments. America sadly needs more
such practical Christians.

These fiery times are but the furnace
in which the gold of true leadership will
be tried, purified, and emerge triumphant.
World evangelization and world peace
await the new leaders who will be equipped
with all the fullness of God's indwelling

power through the complete consecration and utter faith of a Samuel Morris. Where are the Samuel Morrises of today? It is time for new miracle men!

L. J. B.

WOMEN OF FAITH SERIES

Amy Carmichael
Corrie ten Boom
Florence Nightingale
Gladys Aylward
Hannah Whitall Smith
Isobel Kuhn
Joni
Mary Slessor

MEN OF FAITH SERIES

Borden of Yale
Brother Andrew
C. S. Lewis
Charles Finney
Charles Spurgeon
D. L. Moody
Eric Liddell
George Muller
Hudson Taylor
Jim Elliot
Jonathan Goforth
John Hyde
John Newton
John Wesley
Martin Luther
Samuel Morris
Terry Waite
William Carey
William Booth
D. L. Moody

John and Betty Stam